Masters Of Fighting

Presents

THE UNTAUGHT SECRET
TO
MASTERING
SELF-DEFENSE

Protection During
Any Type Of Fighting

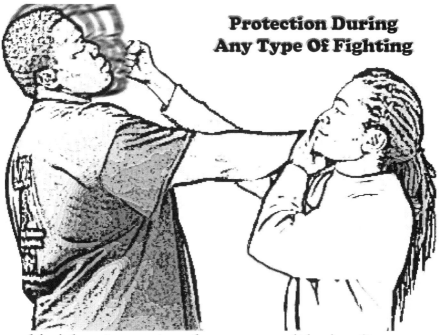

his jab got countered
with a strike to the nose

parry with simultaneous
jab to the nose

For Competition & The Streets
Gary A. Howell, Jr.

Acknowledgment

Special thanks to Eric Howell and Onterryo Barnes for their contributions of time to help illustrate this book. Thanks guys for helping me get my point across. Heartfelt thanks to David Jackson for being an outstanding student and a great friend. Thanks for your continuous motivation.

Disclaimer

Please note that the author and publisher of this book are NOT RESPONSIBLE in any manner whatsoever for any injury that may result from practicing the techniques and/or following the instructions given within. Since physical activities described herein may be too strenuous in nature for some readers to engage in safely, *it is essential that a physician be consulted prior to training.*

Published by Zhandou Dashi, Inc
P.O. Box 13735
Greensboro, North Carolina 27415

ISBN 978-1544879-03-1
ISBN 1-54487-903-2

First edition

Dedication

To all the people who really want to be able to
defend themselves in a real life situation

Preface

Preface

There are tons of products and instructors saying if you use this, you will be able to defend yourself. In most cases, none of these things ever work. Quite frankly, I believe it's not because these things don't work, but because the user does not have the essential secret for achieving the applications properly. I have seen many martial artists who know the forms and even the philosophy of a style of fighting, but are still missing the secret to applying the techniques in a real-life situation. This secret is really a secret that is not told or taught. It is usually learned from many years of practice and sparring. After learning the secret, a person can quickly apply the techniques of any fighting system that they know or will learn. I know because I have helped many people develop the secret with outstanding results. I have had students ranging from seasoned martial artist to the very beginner and they all increased their ability to defend without getting touched. I believe everyone with the intent to defend or fight competitively should know the secret. That is why I put this information together. I took the first lesson that I normally teach students and put it in these pages. In this book, you will find out what the secret is and the fastest process I have found to master it.

Table of Contents

Table of Contents

The First Lesson

This is the first lesson I teach all my students whether it's for self-defense, boxing, or MMA

A Must Have In A Quest To Master Fighting

The Secret

The basis of being able to become great at the act of fighting whether its for competition or self-defense, it starts with having the secret

Most Fighters Don't Know This

The Secret

Don't Tell Nobody

I'm sure you heard of it; you have been doing it since you were born. Think about the times when you were coloring, drawing, writing, or playing with a ball. You were building hand-and-eye coordination.

That is the ability to see and react with your hands. Throughout life, it's important for doing anything that is physical to have a mind-and-body connection. When it comes to self-defense, the connection needed is different. It is more complex. The ability to see and react quickly to avoid injury from another person takes a deeper connection between the mind and body.

Increasing your hand-and-eye coordination to do these tasks will dramatically increase your chances of staying unharmed. Like when you first started playing any sport, you had to build up skill in doing that sport whether it was both physical ability and/or coordination. You got better the more you played. The same thing goes for self-defense.

You need to practice this as realistically as possible so you can quickly get better at doing it. The focus of the first lesson I've taught to all of

3

my students is hand-and-eye coordination. That is the untaught secret.

I have developed a process in tuning this fine motor skill in a safe but realistic way. That does not just increase the reaction time from attacks seen, but also gives the practitioner the ability to shut down the attacker in a matter of seconds. I'm so happy to be sharing this secret with you.

I know you can master self-defense if you are willing to take the time to build your hand-and-eye coordination by doing my process.

the secret

You don't say it

You don't hear it

You don't see it

5

My Process

**It's been used to teach
hundreds of people as their
first lesson since the late 90's**

Guaranteed Results

My Process

Used To Teach Many

In my process, I first teach the student how to do a simple block along with the use of energy while doing this type of block. The simple block I am referring to is traditionally called a parry. Next is a drill to program your subconscious so you can naturally use the parries without having to think about it. These parries are used to redirect an attackers punch, or kick. Keep in mind that a punch or kick are the basic weapons of anyone who would attack you. The next step for the student is to learn a new way to punch. Hand position, use of energy, and the center-line theory are all a part of this step. Then it's time for another drill. In the final step of this process, both the parry and the punch will be used in a drill to program your subconscious to automatically shut down an attacker immediately from their first blow thrown. If you haven't figured it out yet, the purpose of this process is not to just build hand-and-eye coordination efficiently, but as a plus, you build a strong foundation in attack and defense giving you the foundation needed to master fighting.

My Process For This Book

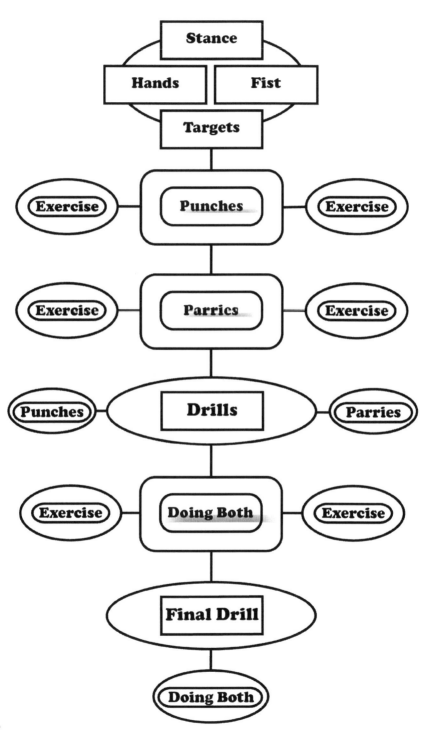

For the purpose of this book, my process has been modified to help you achieve the same results without me being present. The previous illustration shows a chart of the topics in this book. It also shows the order in which it is laid out. There is one thing that has been added to this book that most of my students didn't have to do. That is the exercises. I've added three exercises so you can get the practice needed to achieve the goal of this book.

This is Easy

Mastering This Process

Here's a six step procedure which is very important to achieve the goal of my process

The Plan

Mastering This Process

This Is What You Got To Do

Getting good at physical activities from just a book is really impossible. From a book you can learn information on how to do the physical act, but to get good at it, you have to do it. This process is no different. To get the expected results, you will need to do the following steps. The first step is all mental. It only consist of reading, learning, and basically understand the contents of this book.

Step two is mostly physical. I say mostly physical because the focus here is about doing the physical exercises.

Take A Mental Note

There are three exercises in this book. Two of the exercises consist of punching and parrying, and the other one is being able to do both at the same time.

Step three is finding a person that wants to learn or is willing to help you build hand-eye coordination through this process. I have had students that used their roommate, cousin, brother or sister, girlfriend or boyfriend, and even their husband or wife to master this process. These students took advantage of their time with me, but knew they needed more practice. I actually encouraged them to do so if their hand-eye coordination was very poor. They could not move on to the second lesson until they passed all three tests. After you find the right person, it's time to do the other part. The other part of this step is to teach that person how to parry and punch so they can be your partner in learning to master self-defense.

Step four is doing the first two drills: a parrying drill and a punching drill. One of you will throw punches and the other will parry them. By doing these drills you both will be programing the subconscious on how to parry an attack without thinking. You will also train yourself on how to throw punches and then combos in preparation for a real life situation. During these drills, you also learn how the body moves and the reactions people naturally make.

Step five is about teaching your partner how to punch and parry simultaneously which is the ultimate goal. To be able to defend and attack at the same time will make you so much better at fighting whether it's for sport or self-defense.

The sixth step is the last of the three drills. This is where one of you will throw a punch and the other one will parry and punch simultaneously. Mastering the final drill will bring you both to the highest level of hand-and-eye coordination necessary for mastering fighting.

Steps In Mastering This Process

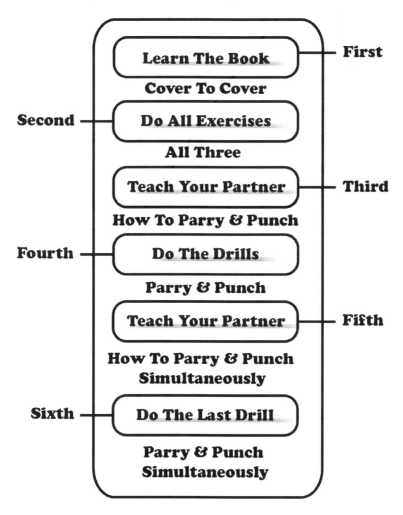

Learn The Book — First
Cover To Cover
Second — Do All Exercises
All Three
Teach Your Partner — Third
How To Parry & Punch
Fourth — Do The Drills
Parry & Punch
Teach Your Partner — Fifth
How To Parry & Punch
Simultaneously
Sixth — Do The Last Drill
Parry & Punch
Simultaneously

The Stance

A good stance in fighting allows for great mobility in attack and defense

In My Process

The Stance

Your Foundation

The stance in any system of fighting is very important. The stance has many benefits such as building the connection to the ground and increasing mobility for attack and defense. For this process, I have students stand in a natural or center stance. I have them start this way because it's the stance they would most likely be in if they had to defend themselves. Also, this stance helps to build a better overall ability for defense because your partner has more of an area to attack. I like to start off by preparing for a real-life situation.

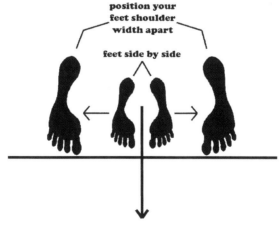

From standing with your feet side by side, spread your feet apart about shoulder width facing your partner.

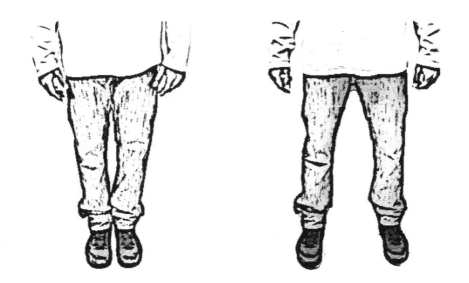

By facing your partner, more of your body is available to try to strike. This will give you the ability to get a wider range of defense. To increase your foundation and mobility, you can bend your knees slightly.

From this position, you will make your legs stronger and more ready to move around when needed. During the first lesson, you do not move at all. The focus here is building hand-eye coordination and simple attack and defense techniques.

the stance in more detail

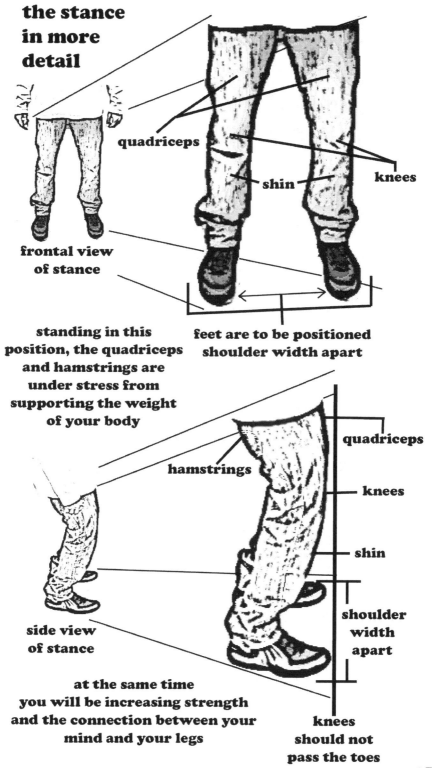

quadriceps

shin

knees

frontal view of stance

standing in this position, the quadriceps and hamstrings are under stress from supporting the weight of your body

feet are to be positioned shoulder width apart

hamstrings

quadriceps

knees

shin

shoulder width apart

side view of stance

at the same time you will be increasing strength and the connection between your mind and your legs

knees should not pass the toes

17

Hand & Arm Position

It's time to learn how to position your arms and hands to increase your ability to attack and defend

Increasing Your Ability

Hand and Arm Position

Allow For Quick Offense & Defense

Your hands and arms are also very important. The position that they are held in should allow for a quicker response of attack and defense techniques.

For this process, your arms and hands will be in a simple on-guard position. You can do this by starting with your arms by your side and palms facing your thighs.

place your arms by your side with your palms facing your thigh

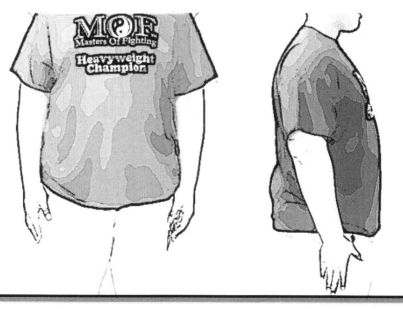

front view　　　　**side view**

Bring your arms in front of you with your elbow about a fist distance from your body.

position arms in front of you with about a fist distance between your body and your elbow

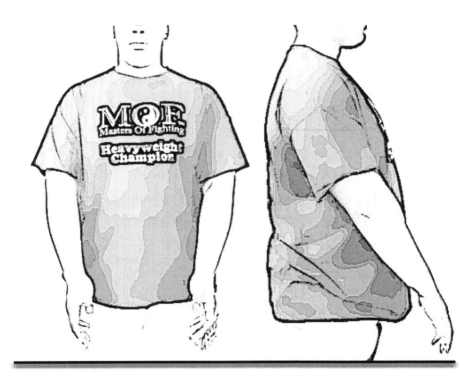

front view   **side view**

Now, bring each of your forearms up at about a forty-five degree angle. At the same time, have your palms facing each other with about twelve inches between them. Your hands should be aligned with the area between your chin and chest.

bring your forearms up to about a 45° angle with your palms facing each other keeping at least twelve inches between them

front view   **side view**

Depending on your partner's height, you may need to bring your hands up or down just a little.

The Fist

It's time to learn how to correctly make a fist and what area to strike with

Your Weapon

The Fist

How To Make & Use Your Weapon

Before we learn how to punch in my process, we first need to focus on making and using the fist safely to avoid injury. I have heard of people breaking a finger or thumb in a fight, especially in self-defense. And this happens usually because the fist wasn't made properly or they hit the attacker with the wrong part of the fist. So, I know it is a need to make sure people understand how to make it and use it. Making a fist correctly involves protecting the fingers and thumb. First, you ball all four of your fingers up to where the tips are pressed in the palm. Then, the thumb is balled up

how to make a fist

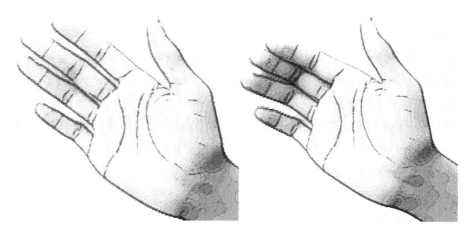

from a open hand

23

bringing the base of the palm to cuff the fingernail while the thumb is pressed against the first two fingers, giving them support and protecting the thumb at the same time.

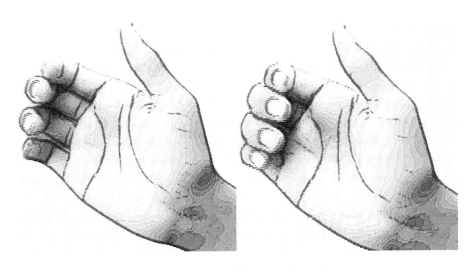

place your finger tips in the middle of your palm

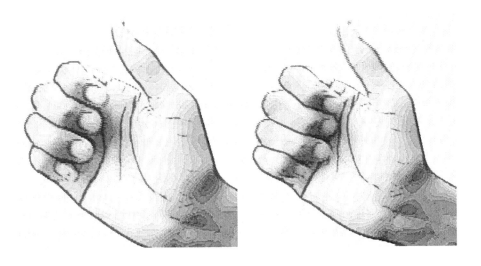

next, you need to protect the thumb by pacing it over the first two fingers, bringing the muscle in palm against the first two finger nails

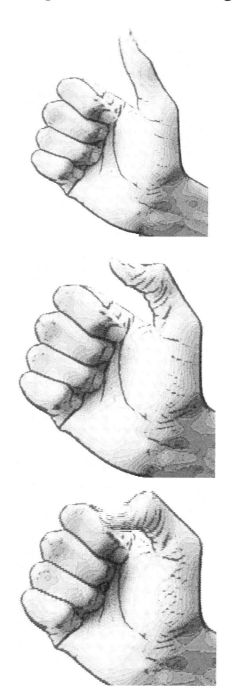

a relaxed fist for going to the target

a tighten fist for striking

That's easy right? Now that you can make a fist, let's get into how it is used. The strongest part of the fist is where the back of the palm and the fingers connect. This area is called the knuckles. The knuckles are great at withstanding human impact without the risk of injury depending on the target area. The first three knuckles (index, middle) have support from the palm and can be used for attack. While the first two knuckles have more support from the thumb making them a stronger weapon. The fourth knuckle (the pinky) does not have any support at all, so, it should never be used to strike with.

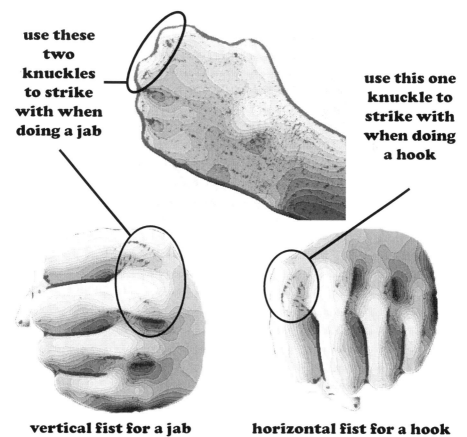

use these two knuckles to strike with when doing a jab

use this one knuckle to strike with when doing a hook

vertical fist for a jab   **horizontal fist for a hook**

The Target Areas

It's time to learn where to aim your strikes

Locations to aim your strikes

The Target Areas

Where To Aim

In mastering self defense, one must know that throwing a hand strike is one of the quickest forms of offense. Think about the time you save because you do not have to reach for a weapon. Actually in fighting, the hand is considered a weapon. With this weapon, there are many types of strikes that can be done from many different angles. This will be broken down in a following book.

In this book, we are focused on building hand-and-eye coordination. And for my process, I like to keep it simple. I only use two types of punches to attack the whole torso: the jab and the hook. With the jab, there are four target areas to strike: the nose, mouth, chest, and abs. With the hook only coming from the side, there

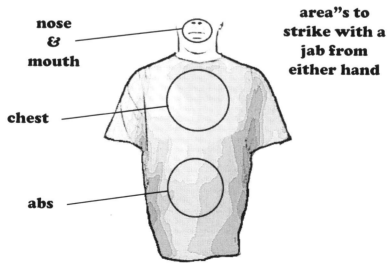

nose
&
mouth

chest

abs

area"s to
strike with a
jab from
either hand

are three areas to strike which is the jaw, ribs, and the obliques.

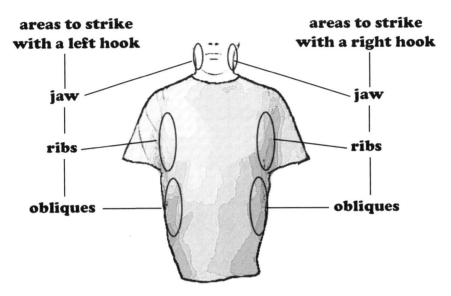

areas to strike with a left hook

areas to strike with a right hook

jaw

jaw

ribs

ribs

obliques

obliques

The center line is a imaginary line going down the center of the body. This is where you will align all of your jabs.

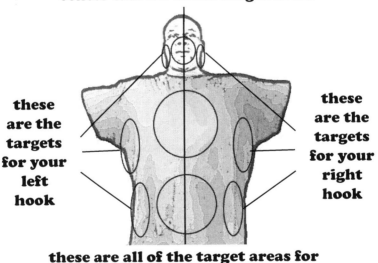

focus your left and right jab on the center line for these target areas

these are the targets for your left hook

these are the targets for your right hook

these are all of the target areas for my process

the jab

top view of your opponent

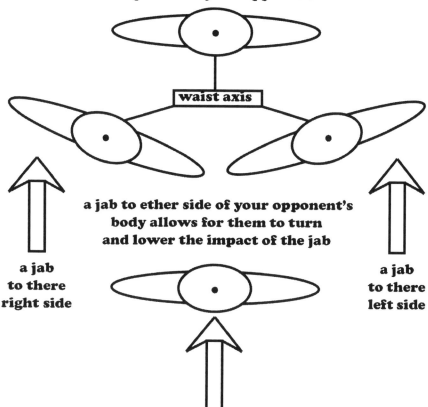

waist axis

a jab to ether side of your opponent's
body allows for them to turn
and lower the impact of the jab

a jab
to there
right side

a jab
to there
left side

a jab to the center of your opponent
results in them feeling all the impact

the hook

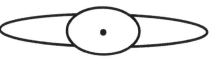

a hook to the side of your
opponent's body results in them
feeling all the impact

a hook
to there
right side

a hook
to there
left side

direction of force

The Punches

It's time to learn how to correctly use the arms to control the fist and the energy involved

How To Attack

The Punches

Controlling Your Weapon

Now that you know where to strike, let's get into how we throw a punch. Since Wing Chun is one of the main systems of fighting I use, I teach people this philosophy of punching. We will start the punch from the on-guard position previously discussed.

the on-guard position

(1) In my process, all punches comes from the on-guard position. You can think of this as the ready position

33

For a jab, you flex the deltoid and triceps muscles to throw a relaxed arm and vertical fist to the target area. If the target has not moved or the punch is not redirected, you tighten up your arm and fist upon impact. Then, quickly relax.

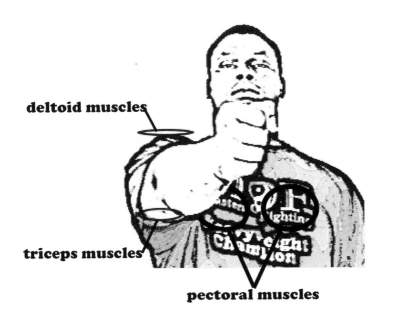

deltoid muscles

triceps muscles

pectoral muscles

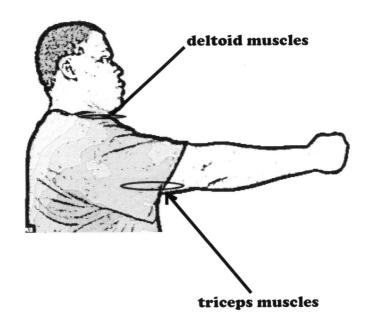

deltoid muscles

triceps muscles

The left jab from the on-guard position

(2) at the start of the left jab, you begin to ball the fist up

(3) with your fist balled up, but not tighten, you throw your fist at the target area

(4) you keep your fist and all the muscle in your arm relaxed

(5) upon impact, you tighten your fist and arm (deltoid, triceps, and pectoral muscles)

(6) then, relax the fist and arm immediately

(7) bring the arm and hand back into the on-guard position (using biceps, and upper back muscles)

(8) stay relaxed

(9) back into the on-guard position

38

The right jab from the on-guard position

10

(10) at the start of the right jab, you begin to ball the fist up

11

(11) with your fist balled up, but not tighten, you throw your fist at the target area

(12) you keep your fist and all the muscle in your arm relaxed

(13) upon impact, you tighten your fist and arm (deltoid, triceps, and pectoral muscles) then relax

(14) bring the arm and hand back into the on-guard position (using biceps, and upper back muscles)

(15) stay relaxed

16

(16) back into the on-guard position

target areas for the jab

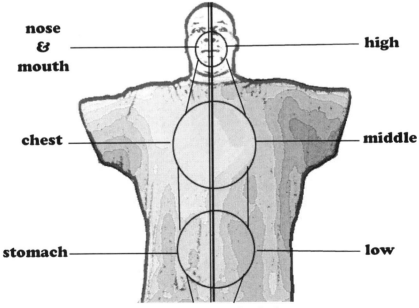

nose & mouth — high

chest — middle

stomach — low

left and right jab down the center

right jab to the nose   **left jab to the nose**

right jab to the chest   **left jab to the chest**

right jab to the stomach   **left jab to the stomach**

43

For the hook, you flex the middle deltoid muscle bringing your elbow up. At the same time, you flex the triceps muscles moving your relaxed fist in a loop to strike the targets on the side. After your fist goes out far as you want it to go, then, flex the biceps, frontal deltoids, and connecting pectoral muscles bringing your vertical fist to a horizontal fist by the time it reaches the target. Remember, that you only tighten the fist upon impact.

The right hook from the on-guard position

the on-guard position

(2) at the start of the right hook, you begin to ball up the fist

(3) with your fist balled up, but not tighten, you use your deltoid muscles to bring your elbow up

(4) continue to bring your elbow up while using the triceps to move your forearm outward

(5) while bringing your elbow up, align your fist with your elbow

46

(6) stop bringing your elbow up when you're at the height needed to reach the target area

(7) stop bringing your forearm out so that your fist doesn't pass your elbow; then, using your muscles, throw your fist at the target area

8

(8) relax all your muscles except for those in your forearm because you turn your fist horizontally before hitting the target area

9

(9) while on the way to your target area, try not to use any unnecessary energy

(10) you will still use your muscles to guide the fist to it's destination

(11) upon impact, you tighten up all necessary muscles even in your waist

(12) after impact, you relax all your muscles while retracting your arm

(13) bringing your elbow back down while opening your fist

(14) remember to stay relaxed while
dropping the elbow back into
the on-guard position

(15) once the elbow is a fist distance from
your body, move the hand into position

16

(16) still in a relaxed state, move the
hand into the on-guard position

17

(17)arm and hand back in the
on-guard position

The left hook from the on-guard position

(18) start in the on-guard position

(19) at the start of the left hook, you begin to ball up the fist

(20) with your fist balled up but not tighten, you use your deltoid muscles to bring your elbow up

(21) continue to bring your elbow up while using the triceps to move your forearm outward

(22) while bringing your elbow up, align your fist with your elbow

**(23) use your forearm muscles to
turn your fist horizontally**

**(24) stop bringing your elbow up when you reach the
height needed to hit the target area, stop bringing your
forearm out so that your fist doesn't pass your elbow**

(25) using the necessary muscles, throw your fist at the target area

(26) while on the way to your target area try not to use any unnecessary energy

(27) you will still use your muscles to guide the fist to its destination

(28) upon impact, you tighten up all necessary muscles even in your waist

(29) after impact, you relax all your muscles while retracting your arm

(30) bringing your elbow back down while opening your fist

(31) remember to stay relaxed

**(32) remember to stay relaxed while
dropping the elbow back into
the on-guard position**

(33) once the elbow is a fist distance from your body, move the hand into position

(34) arm and hands back into the on-guard position

Target areas for the hook

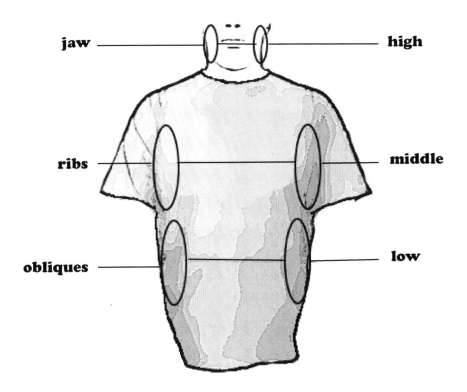

jaw — high

ribs — middle

obliques — low

While doing the drills in my process, you should never hit your partner or tighten up your fist. I have found that by practicing this form of control throughout training will build up more explosive power in a real-life situation.

right hook to the jaw   **left hook to the jaw**

right hook to the rib   **left hook to the rib**

right hook to the oblique   **left hook to the oblique**

63

Exercise One

It's time to get a physical and visual understanding of throwing a punch correctly including learning to master the use of energy

Throwing Punches

The First Exercise

Practicing Throwing The Punches

This exercise is all about programming the subconscious with the ability to throw a punch. I believe that before you should get to do it in a drill or have to do it in a real-life situation, you should be familiar on how to throw a punch correctly. A punch thrown correctly can only be achieved through understanding it and only mastered by practicing it. In this exercise, you are going to get both: the understanding and little practice. A lot more practice will come later. Just so you know, I am saying "throwing punches" because that is actually what you are doing, throwing a relaxed fist to a specific target.

For the purpose of this book, I designed all three exercises so, you can do it by yourself and still improve your offence dramatically. When I train my students, I'm there to teach and guide them to reach destination. Now, you must take the wheel and steer yourself to the destination. In order for you to arrive to the same place, there are a few things I want you to keep in mind while you do this exercise.

The first and foremost thing you should keep in mind is how you use your energy. Think of your energy as if it was coming from a battery placed in your stomach and when the battery dies, all your energy is gone. Plus, check this out! For wasting

65

energy, the consequence will be your battery dying much quicker. That is something to think about. In fact, that is just how our bodies operate. The more muscle we use, the faster we get tired. You don't want to get tired, right? So, you should stay conscious of how you use energy and its preservation.

The second thing to keep in mind is speed. How fast can you throw a punch? One of the requirements of self-defense and competition fighting is that you are faster than your opponent. Being faster makes the situation a whole lot easier. I teach my students how increase the speed of their punches by only using the muscles to throw the fist to the target and then to quickly retract it. That will not just make your punches faster, but will, also, allow you to reserve energy. Get to know how fast you can throw a punch.

The third thing to keep in mind is distance. I'm talking about the distance from the start of the punch to the point of impact. Misjudging the distance in a real-life situation could make you vulnerable to get hit by an attack. You also could be swinging at the air. To make sure that will never happen, visually pay attention to the distance your fist goes when throwing punches. See how far your fist can go with your arm fully extended. After practicing, all that information from your sight will be stored in your brain. Then, you will know the distance your fist can strike.

The fourth thing to keep in mind is timing. Timing in throwing punches is a very complex topic. It has so many levels. Timing applies from the moment you throw a punch to the time you throw another. It could also be applied at the time the fist hits the target. If you think about it, in between start to finish of a punch you got distance and speed. So, to keep it simple, think of timing as rhythm. You would not want your opponent to know your rhythm because that will make your punches predictable. So play with the timing and try to keep your strikes unexpected.

The fifth and final thing to keep in mind is combinations. A combination is done when you combine punches together. It can be two or more, and by linking them together increases your level of attack. So, the more the merrier. I can land thirty or more punches in three seconds. This may sound impossible, but it's actually quite easy with the right training and use of energy.

This exercise has two parts. The first part is where you practice on throwing punches in a place where you have privacy to focus. The other part is throwing punches in the front of a mirror. These two parts are essential to increase your ability to attack in future drills and in a real-life situation. So, let's get started. From the on-guard position, in a relaxed state with very calm breathing, throw punches in no certain order aiming at an imaginary target. Remember all nine of the target areas. Throw all your punches at them areas. Jabs to the center of the target and hooks to the side of the target. You are to do this part of the exercise for at least three minutes. You are to get familiar with throwing punches. The following are illustrations showing a person doing the first part of the punching exercise.

70

The previous illustrations from number (1) to (70) show a simple twelve strike combination starting from on-guard position and ending in the on-guard position that attacks all nine of the target ares during the first part of the punching exercise. This is only a sample showing what it looks like to do this exercise. You can double or triple up on the jab before or after throwing multiple hooks to the body. There is no set punching combination. You are free to explore all possibilities you can achieve with your fist.

The second part is done by standing in the on-guard position about three or four feet facing the mirror. The mirror needs to be large enough to see your whole upper body. You begin this exercise in the on-guard position, and start throwing punches with each hand.

While throwing the punches, you want to pay close attention to your reflection in the mirror. Make sure you watch the movement of the fist, arm, and torso during every punch you throw. This will actually educate you on what it would look like when someone else attacks you. Visually seeing these movements prepares you to have a quicker response for when that time comes.

By the way, there is no specific time to do this exercise. Although, my suggestion is you do at least all twelve of the punches used in my process three times. They are the left and right jab to the nose, chest, and stomach, Plus, the left and right hook to the jaw, ribs, and obliques.

You want to make sure that you're making your fist correctly, and using the right knuckles as if you were going to hit each target. At the same time, continue to focus on mastering the use of energy by using the muscle to just throw the fist at the target, tensing up only at the split second of would-be impact, and then, quickly relaxing.

The following is some illustrations showing you what it should look like to do this exercise in front of a mirror. The illustrations are in a certain order, but you should keep your punches random. Don't forget to practice your combinations and have fun.

**standing in the on-guard position
in front of the mirror**

**throwing a left jab from the on-guard position
in front of the mirror**

in front of the mirror in the on-guard position

left jab to the nose from the on-guard position

left jab to the chest from the on-guard position

in front of the mirror in the on-guard position

right jab to the nose from the on-guard position

right jab to the chest from the on-guard position

**left jab
to the
stomach
from the
on-guard
position**

**left hook
to the jaw
from the
on-guard
position**

**left hook
to the ribs
from the
on-guard
position**

**right jab
to the
stomach
from the
on-guard
position**

**right hook
to the jaw
from the
on-guard
position**

**right hook
to the ribs
from the
on-guard
position**

85

left hook to the obliques from the on-guard position

hands-together bow is a simple gesture that shows modesty and respect

right hook to the obliques from the on-guard position

hands-together bow is a simple gesture that shows modesty and respect

The Parries

It's time to learn how to correctly do a simple block and how to control the energy involved

The Simple Block

The Parries

Understanding Your Defense

All martial arts systems have blocking techniques that are used to deflect an attack of an opponent. There are basically two ways energy is used while doing a block. One way is using lots of energy and the other way is using minimum energy. In relationship to martial arts systems, you have hard styles and soft styles. I am not in favor of the hard styles. I started practicing martial arts with hard styles and realized they stress the use of too much movement and energy by having the practitioner doing more than what is needed.

This way of defense and attack makes it impossible to beat a person who is faster and not wasteful with energy. I, also, feel that these types of systems are harder to work for self-defense in the beginning. For these reasons, when creating this process to build hand-eye coordination, I wanted the practitioner to immediately be able to defend oneself in a real situation. So, parries are the only type of defense used in this process.

Parries minimize the use of energy and movement. It is a natural body movement, so natural in fact, fighters with no martial arts training would do a parry to avoid getting hit, especially boxers. But since they do not practice on how to do a parry correctly, in most cases, the use of energy is still very high.

The outcome of this wasteful use of energy makes the fighter slow and tired. Being inefficient at using energy is one the first signs of not being a master. A parry really is what you would call any simple block. - I first learned of a parry by Bruce Lee, then, later found out people have been doing parries since they started defending. That's a very long time. There are basically four parries done with each hand.

The four right hand parry positions

right hand parry	right hand parry
to redirect a left jab to the face or chest	to redirect a left hook to the face

right hand parry　　　**right hand parry**

to redirect a low left
jab or kick to the abs
or groin

to redirect a left hook
or kick to the obliques
and to the hip

The four left hand parry positions

left hand parry　　　**left hand parry**

to redirect a right jab
to the face or chest

to redirect a right hook
to the face

left hand parry   **left hand parry**

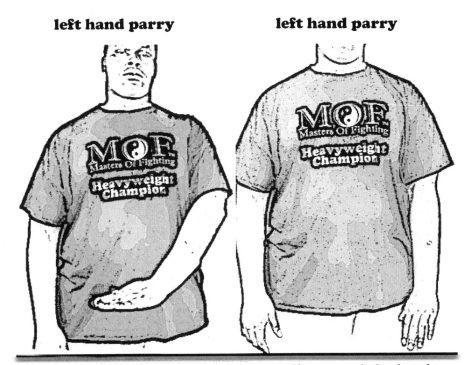

to redirect a low right jab or kick to the abs or groin   **to redirect a right hook or kick to the obliques and to the hip**

So there are eight parry positions all together. Each position defends a specific type of attack to the torso. A parry should be done at the last moment before the attacker would get the strike which is about three to six inches before impact. A parry is also done from a relaxed state. Then muscle is used to throw the forearm into the parry position. At the moment you are about to redirect the attack, you tighten up your hand and then quickly relax your muscles to get ready for the next movement.

right parry for high left jab   **left parry for high right jab**

right parry for high left hook   **left parry for high right hook**

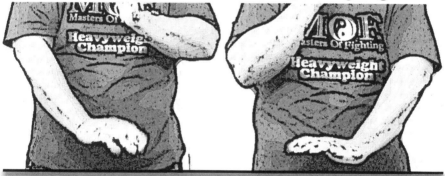

right parry for low left jab   **left parry for low right jab**

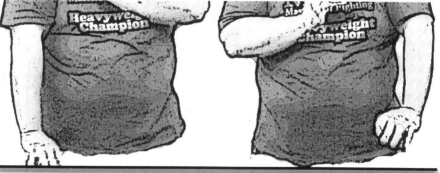

right parry for low left hook   **left parry for low right hook**

Exercise
Two

It's time to get a physical and visual understanding of doing parries correctly including learning to master the use of energy

Doing Parries

The Second Exercise

Practicing The Parries

During this exercise, you will practice doing a parry. This exercise also has two parts. The first part is done in front of a mirror. The second part is done anywhere you are comfortable with your eyes closed.

You will do the first part by standing in a natural stances about three or four feet facing the mirror. The mirror needs to be large enough to see yourself doing all four of the parries with each hand. Ideally, you want to be able to see your whole torso, from the top of your head and a few inches outside of both shoulders down to below your waist.

You begin this exercise in the on-guard position, and imagine that someone is throwing all twelve punches at you. Start doing all the parries with each hand to defend yourself. While doing the parries, you want to pay close attention to the form, making sure that your energy is used correctively by not tensing up until the point of would-be impact and stopping your hand with your thumb, palm, and fingers in the right position. I suggest you do this first part of the exercise for at least three minutes as you try to perfect the use of energy and correct hand position. The following is some illustrations of what it would look like to be practicing in front of the mirror.

in front
of the
mirror
in the
on-guard
position

left parry
to defend
against a
left hook to the
jaw from the
on-guard
position

left parry
to defend
against a
left jab to the
face from the
on-guard
position

in front
of the
mirror
in the
on-guard
position

right parry
to defend
against a
right hook to the
jaw from the
on-guard
position

right parry
to defend
against a
right jab to the
face from the
on-guard
position

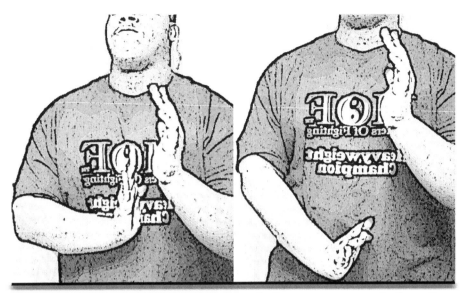

left parry to defend against a left jab to the chest from the on-guard position

left parry to defend against a left jab to the stomach from the on-guard position

left parry to defend against a left hook to the obliques from the on-guard position

hands-together bow is a simple gesture that shows modesty and respect

right parry to defend against a right jab to the chest from the on-guard position

right parry to defend against a right jab to the stomach from the on-guard position

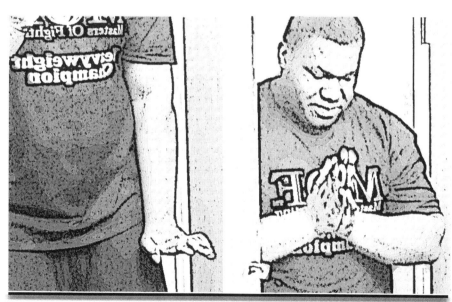

right parry to defend against a right hook to the obliques from the on-guard position

hands-together bow is a simple gesture that shows modesty and respect

When doing the second part of this exercise, you will also need to imagine someone standing in front of you throwing all twelve punches. Forcing you to do all six parries with each hand to redirect their punches. Your focus in this part of the exercise should be on speed, form, and control. The following is illustrations of a master doing the second part of this exercise. It's not here for you to copy, but just to give you an idea of what it should look like.

102

17

18

19

20

21

22

104

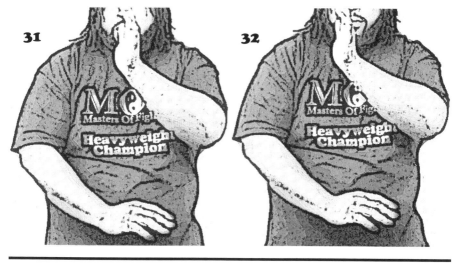

105

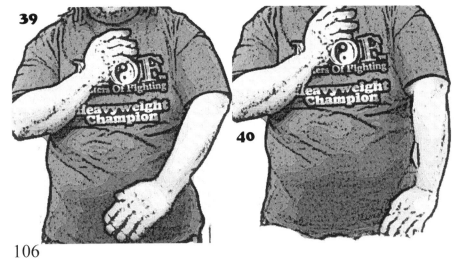

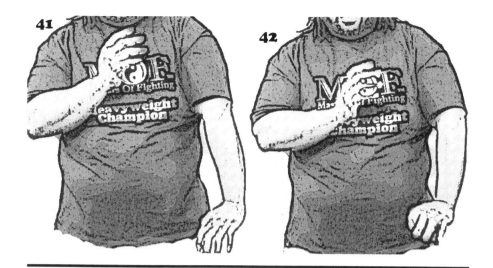

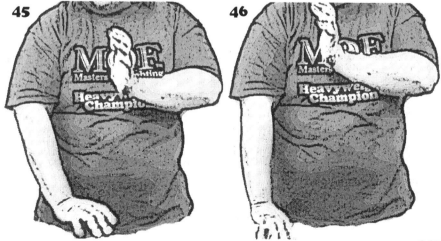

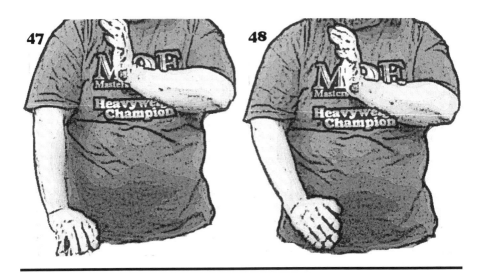

109

111

71  72

73  74

75  76

In the previous illustrations, from (1) to (92) show a simple run through of the second exercise using most of the parries. He is practicing his defense against a jab to the face, chest, and stomach, along with the defense against a hook to the face and body. He is starting from the on-guard position and ending in the on-guard position. Remember, this is only a sample showing what it looks like to do this exercise. Don't forget to imagine someone is attacking you, forcing you to redirect their punches. Additionally, you can double or triple up on a certain parry because the attacks could come that way.

Building Your Defense

Now it's time to build your ability to see an attack and defend it without thinking while mastering the use of energy involved

Parring Without Thinking

Building Your Defense

The First Drill

The first drill we would do is to build up your defense. Learning to defend an attack without thinking is essential to mastering fighting. In this drill, you train your eyes to see an attack. At the same time, you learn about distance, timing, speed, and how to use your energy. We would start in a neutral stance about a fist distance from each other in the on-guard position. I would start throwing punches at you, not with the intentions of hitting, but to stop about three inches from impact. Using only jabs and hooks with both hands, I would throw punches at your whole torso starting out very slow to make sure you understand how to do all the parries. Then, I would slowly increase the speed while changing the timing of the punches. As your eyes and reaction time adjust, you will be training your subconscious to defend any attack you see without thinking. You are immediately increasing your hand-eye coordination.

On-guard Position

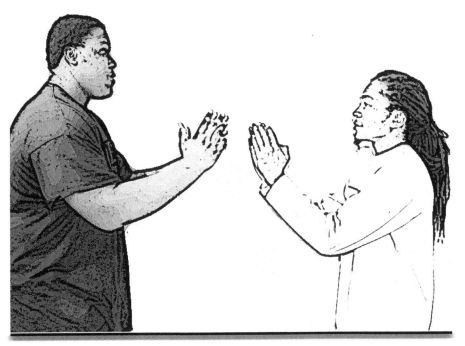

side view

Parring the left jab to the mouth

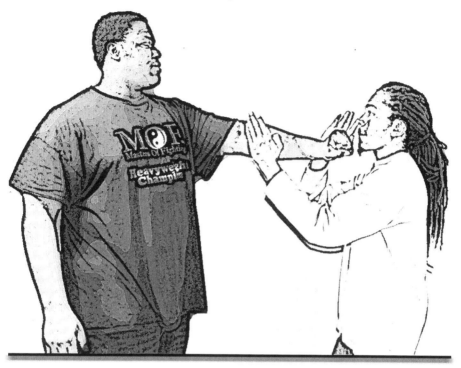

side view

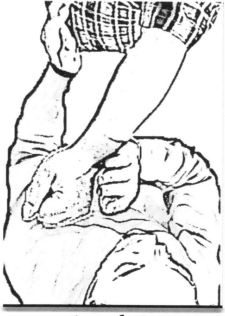

top view

119

Parring the right jab to the mouth

side view

top view

Parring the left hook to the jaw

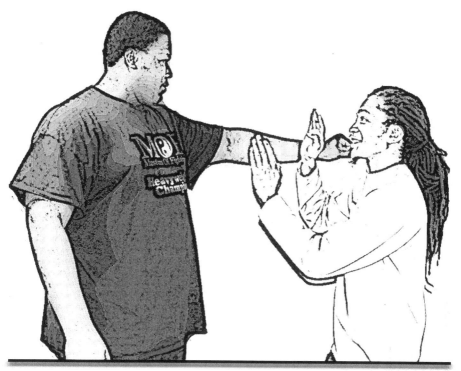

side view

top view

121

Parring the right hook to the jaw

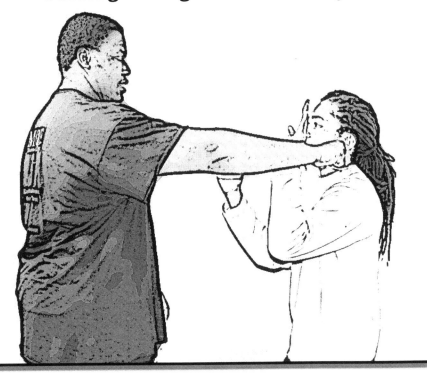

side view

top view

Parring the left jab to the stomach

side view

top view

123

Parring the right jab to the stomach

side view

top view

Parring the left kick or hook to the obliques

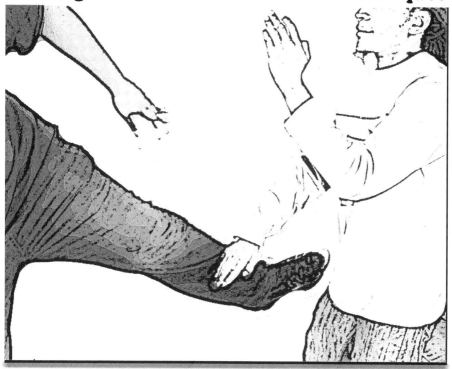

side view

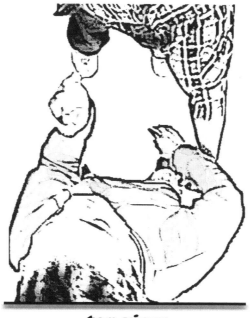

top view

125

Parring the right kick or hook to the stomach

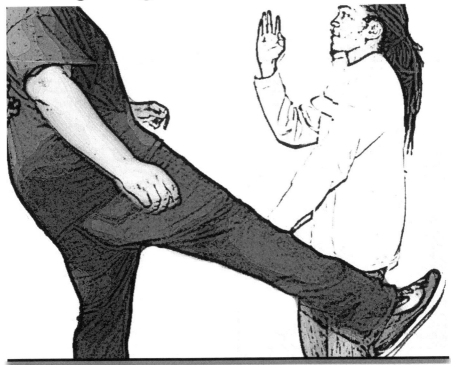

side view

top view

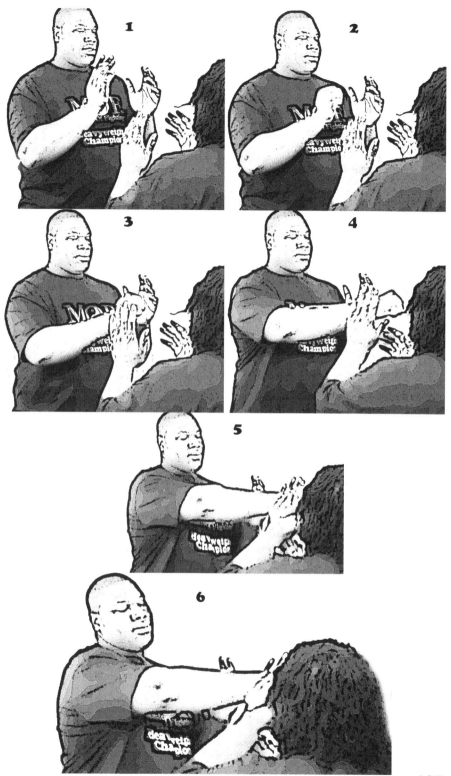

127

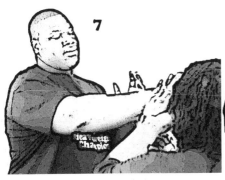

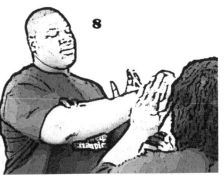

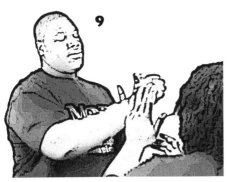

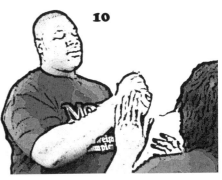

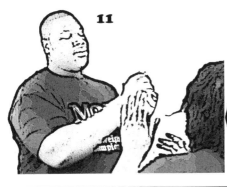

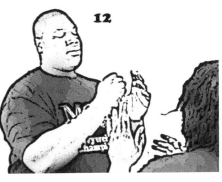

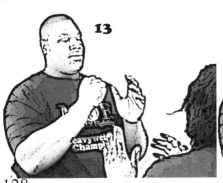

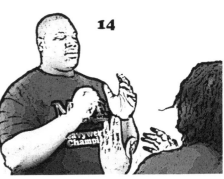

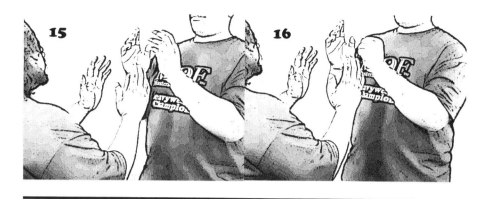

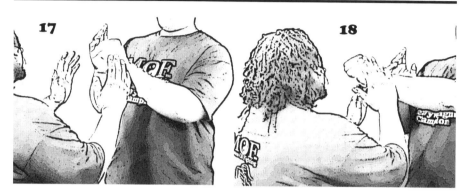

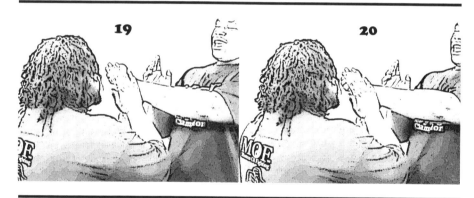

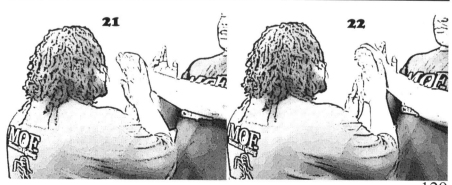

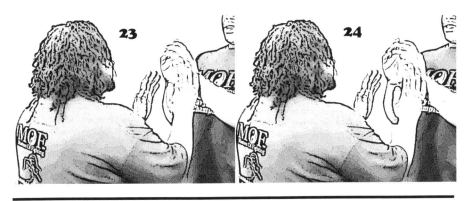

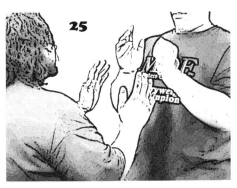

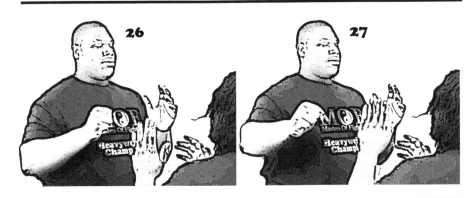

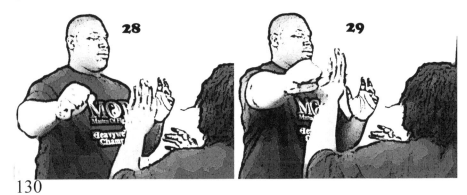

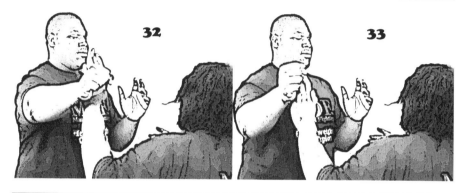

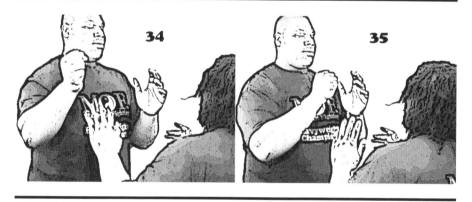

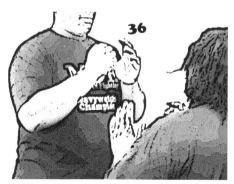

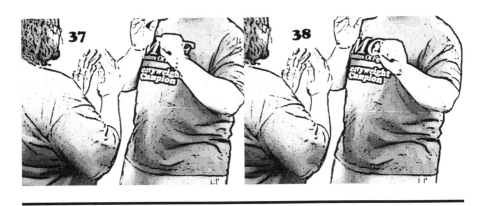

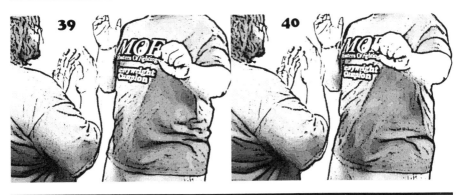

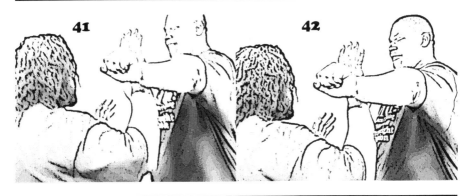

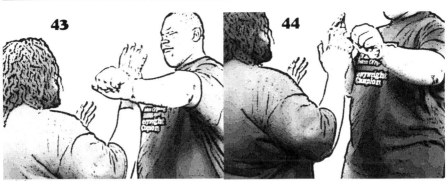

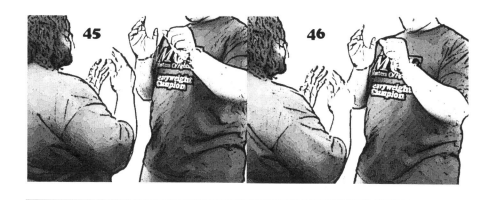

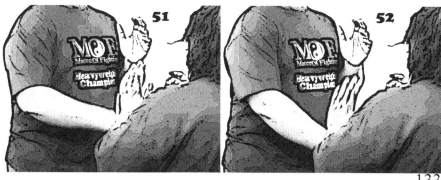

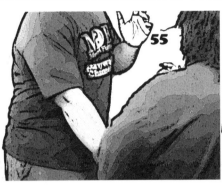

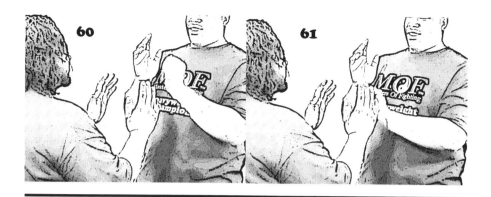

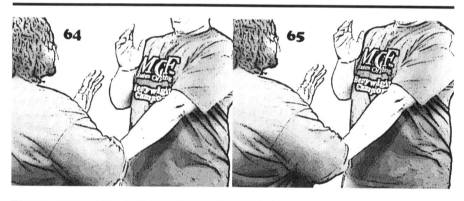

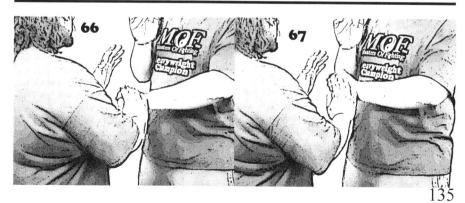

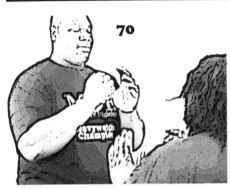

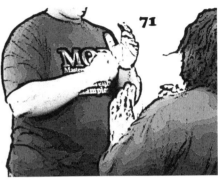

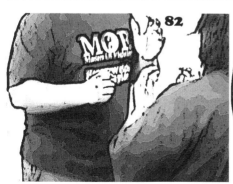
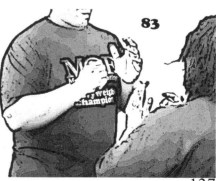

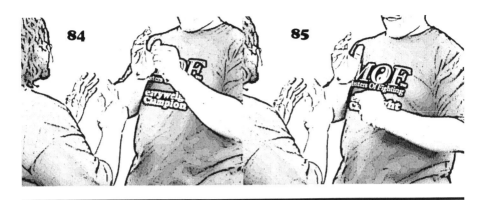

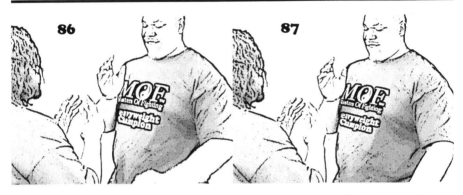

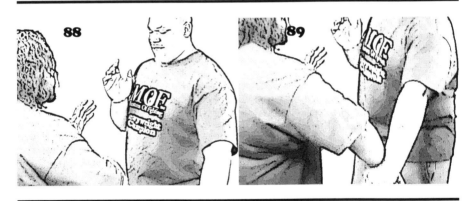

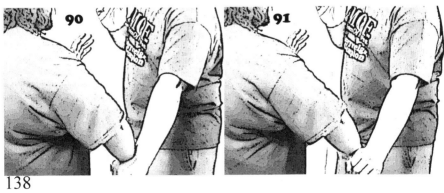

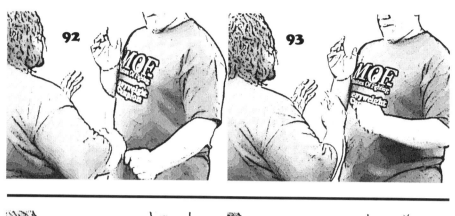

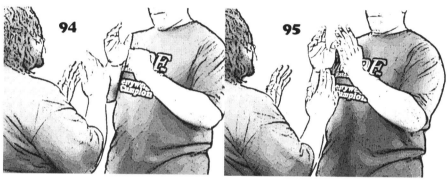

In the previous illustrations from (1) to (95) show a simple run through of the first drill using only four attacks and parries with each hand. The jab to the chest and hook to the ribs are not shown. These illustrations are just to give you an idea of what it should look like. The focus here is to build the ability to defend. In doing so, you need to learn the movements of the body before and during an attack. At the same time, get to know your reaction time. Pay close attention to the timing and distance of each attack. All this practice with a real person will dramatically pay off in your ability to defend. As the attacker in this drill, your focus should be on helping your partner get better at defense.

Remember to always stay relaxed when throwing punches. You should, also, start off slow, and then gradually pick up speed as their defense gets better. The person throwing punches will also benefit in this drill.

Building Your Offense

Now it's time to build your ability to see an opening to attack while mastering the use of energy involved

Punching Through Their Defense

Building Your Offense

The Second Drill

The second drill we would do will be used to build up your offense. Learning to attack properly is the key to controlling the situation. In this drill, you will be building your combinations, speed, and accuracy that will result in you creating explosive power, as well as, you mastering the overall use of energy, timing, distance. I would have you start the same as before, about a fist distance from me in an on-guard hand position from the neutral stance. Now, I would have you throw jabs and hooks at me starting off slowly and then gradually getting faster to help build your hand-eye coordination. In this drill, you will focus on attacking open areas of the torso. While throwing punches, play around with different combinations and change up the timing. Get used to throwing punches and remember to focus on stopping each strike three inches before impact, because you are not striking, you are building up your control, which intern builds up explosive power. So, when you must strike, it won't take many.

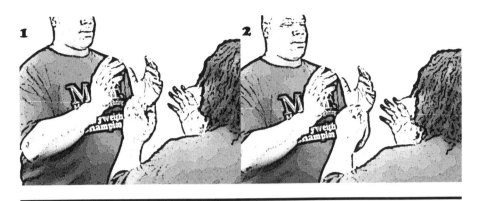

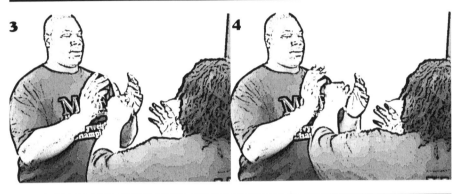

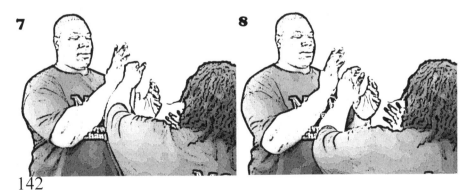

142

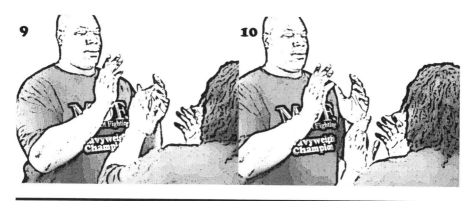

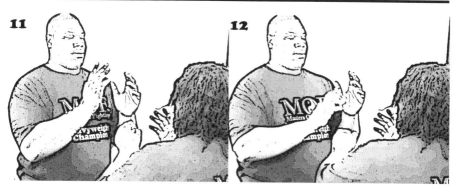

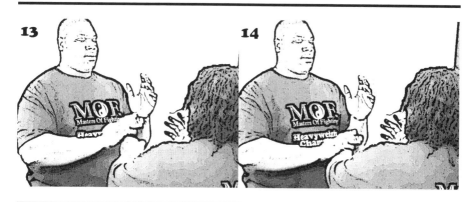

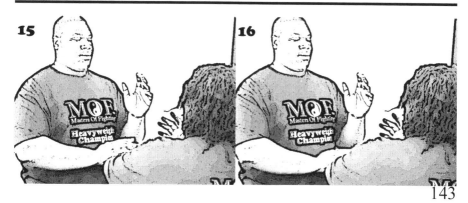

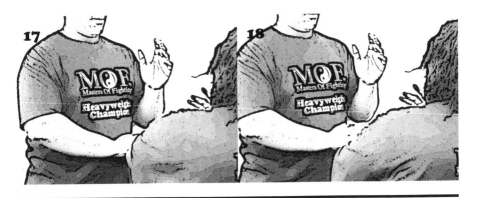

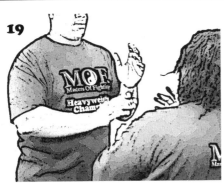

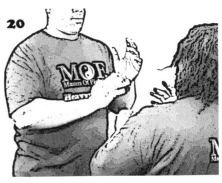

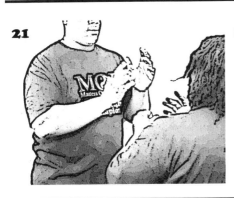

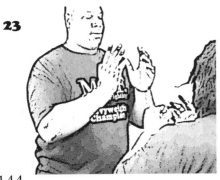

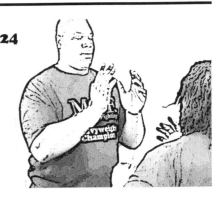

144

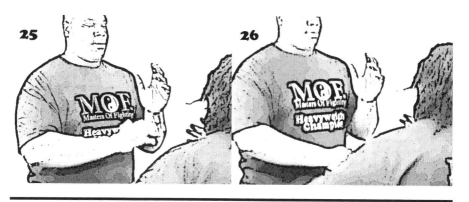

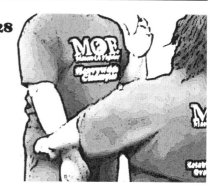

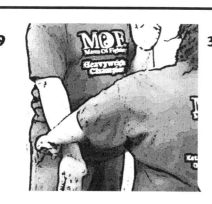

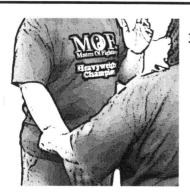

145

34

35

36

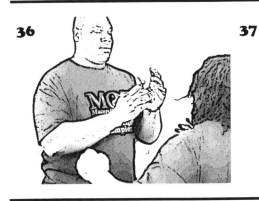

37

38

39

40

41

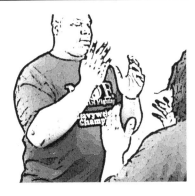

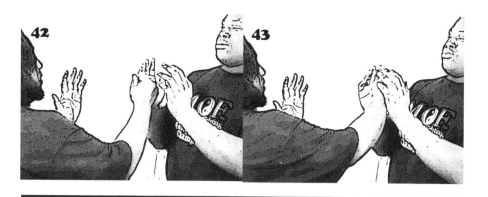

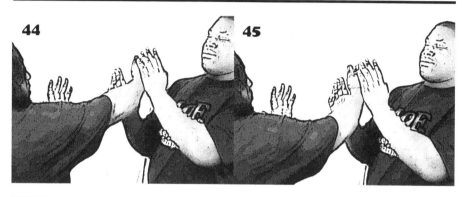

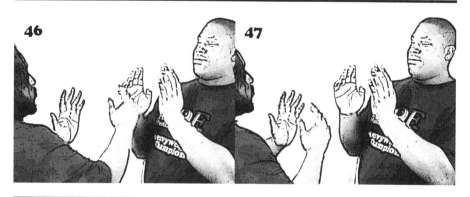

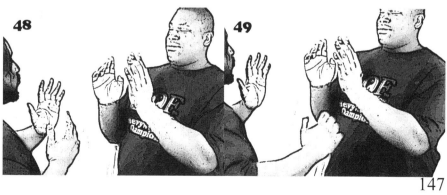

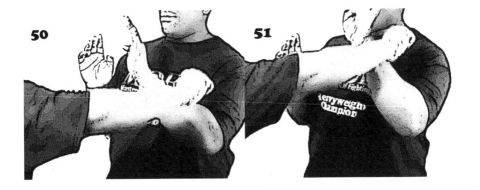

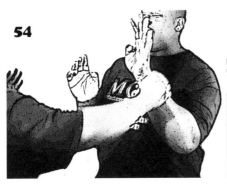

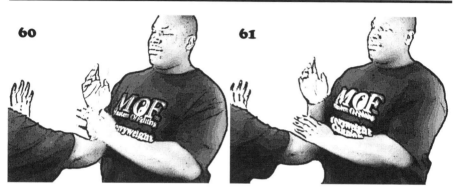

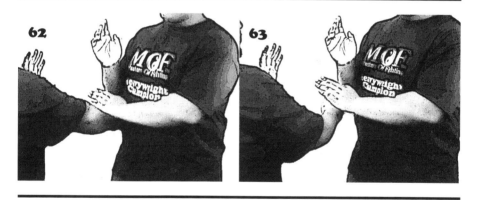

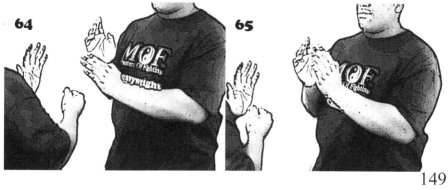

149

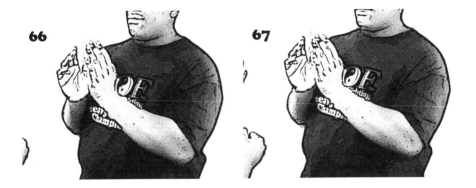

66   67

68   69

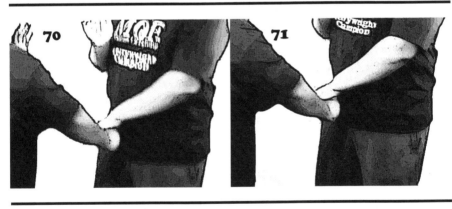

70   71

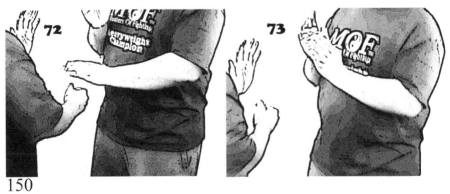

72   73

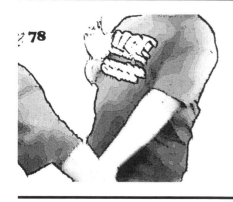

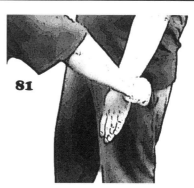

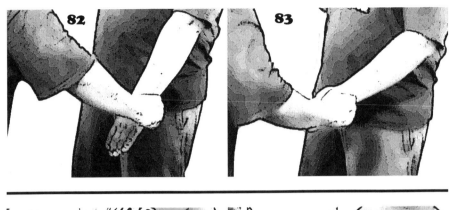

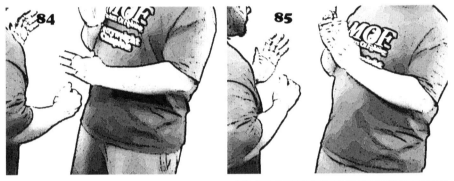

Target Area's

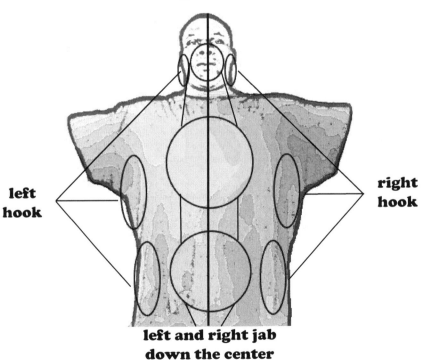

left hook

right hook

left and right jab down the center

152

Combining Them Together

Now it's time to learn how to combine your offense and defense simultaneously

Attack and Defend at the Same Time

Combining Them Together

Parrying with the Simultaneous Punch

The parry with the simultaneous punch is just as it sounds. This is where the defense and the offense are done at the same time. Or you can say offense and defense because in a fight, it can go either way. In my opinion, this is the second fastest way to counter a punch. I think the fastest is bobbing or weaving with a strike but that takes more energy and physical fitness. Now back to the topic, I found that doing a parry and a punch at the same time will multiply the penetration of the punch because the attacker is moving into it. So, the impact of a strike will be unexpected. In a real-life situation, this will cause quick knockouts or the attacker to quickly be shut down. This changes the game in self-defense and competition bringing more control of the confrontation and minimizing the danger.

left hand parry with a simultaneous right jab to the nose

the left hand could parry any right jab to the face

right hand parry with a simultaneous left jab to the nose

the right hand could parry any left jab to the face

left hand parry with a simultaneous right hook to the jaw

the left hand could parry a right hook to the jaw or ribs

right hand parry with a simultaneous left hook to the jaw

the right hand could parry a left hook to the jaw or ribs

left hand parry with a simultaneous right jab to the stomach

the left hand could parry a right jab to the stomach

right hand parry with a simultaneous left jab to the stomach

the right hand could parry a left jab to the stomach

left hand parry with a simultaneous right hook to the obliques

the left hand could parry a right hook or kick to the obliques

right hand parry with a simultaneous left hook to the obliques

the right hand could parry a left hook or kick to the obliques

Exercise
Three

It's time to get a physical and visual understanding of doing both simultaneously including learning to master the use of energy

Doing Both Simultaneously

The Third Exercise

Practicing Offense & Defense Simultaneously

In this exercise, you will practice on parrying and punching at the same time. I think that having the ability to do this in a real-life situation will not only guarantee a knockout or shut them down, but will also show one of the highest levels of hand-and-eye coordination when it comes to fighting. Think about it. To defend and attack at the same time in a situation is so much faster than doing a typical counter, that's where you would weave or block, then, try to strike the attacker. Blocking then trying to strike someone will only give them time to recover from their inability to strike you. What I mean by this is, there could be more attacks you will have to block and more chances of you getting hit. When doing a parry with a simultaneous punch, the attacker moves into the punch making the impact of your punch much greater. To be able to do this in a real situation takes a higher level of practice. And it's coming! But first you need to warm your mind and body up with this exercise. This exercise only has one part so, a mirror is not needed. You will start in the on-guard position as normal then; imagine someone throwing random jabs and hooks at all nine target areas on you. With every imaginary attack, you are to do a parry and a simultaneous punch. There's no time limit. Just get comfortable doing them together.

166

7

8

9

10

11

12

13

14

15

16

17

18

25

26

27

28

29

30

31

32

33

34

35

36

171

37

38

39

40

41

42

172

43

44

45

46

47

48

49

50

51

52

53

54

55

56

57

58

59

60

73

74

75

76

77

78

The previous illustrations from (1) to (82) show the master defending imaginary attacks with eight different parries, each including a simultaneous punch. He started from and finished in the on-guard position. The parries and punches match the punches thrown from the imaginary attacker. You should be able to tell by looking at the simultaneous parry and punch, and noticing that they match each other. Just so you know, the fastest simultaneous punch is the jab. These illustrations are just a sample showing what it looks like to do this exercise. When you do this exercise, remember to make sure that your parries and punches are done correctly.

Building Your Ability To Do Both

Now it's time to build your
ability to parry and punch
while mastering
the use of energy involved

Punch and Parry

The Third Drill

Having the ability to defend and attack simultaneously in a serious situation is a skill that most people don't have. I have seen a lot of MMA and boxing events, where approximately ninety percent of the fighters, to me, didn't have good hand-eye coordination. In addition, most of them cannot attack and defend simultaneously.

After programming the subconscious with this drill, all that will come without thinking. This drill has the highest level of hand-eye coordination training for self-defense and competition fighting. It will be that game changer that put you on higher level than most.

Now, let's get started. We would start in the neutral stance about a fist distance from each other and hands in the on-guard position. Then, I would start throwing punches at you extremely slow. You will parry just like before, but now you would, also, throw a jab at the same time. The goal is to have already be stopped three inches before impact with your punch at the same time your parry begin to touch the wrist of their punch. This ability does not come easy, so, you will have to build up to it.

As you get better, I would increase the speed and change the timing of my punches. This will give you the capability to adapt better in a real-life

181

situation because you will know the body movements, your reaction time will be faster, plus, you can attack while defending.

On-guard Position

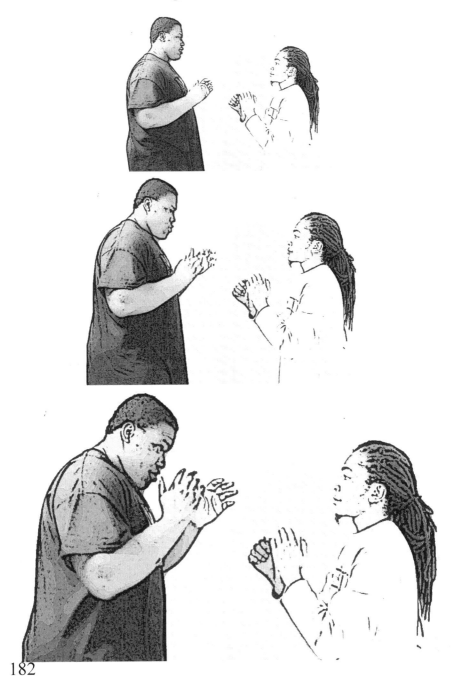

183

Parrying the left hook to the jaw with a simultaneous right jab

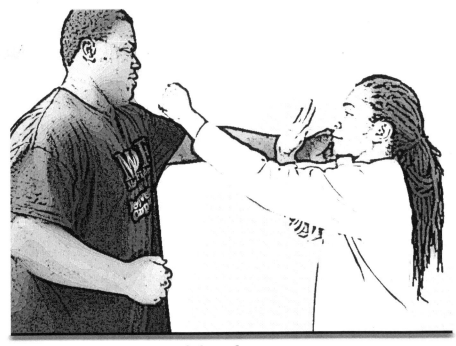

side view

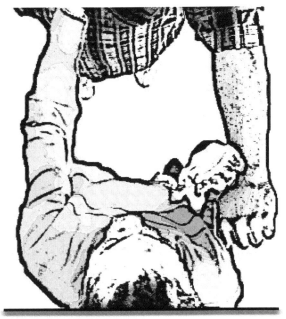

top view

Parrying the right hook to the jaw with a simultaneous left jab

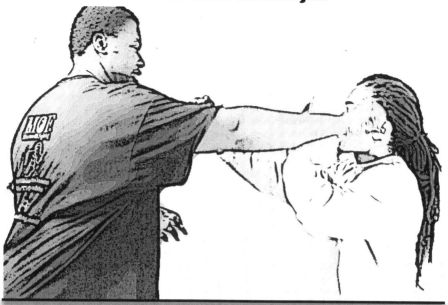

side view

top view

185

Parrying the left jab to the nose with a simultaneous right jab

side view

top view

Parrying the right jab to the nose with a simultaneous left jab

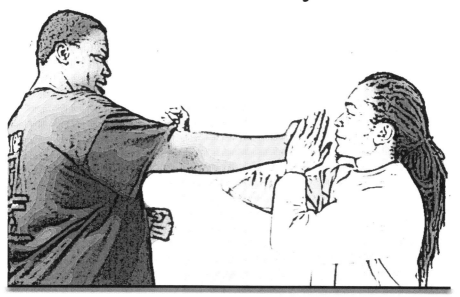

side view

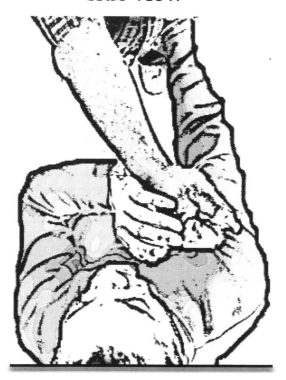

top view

187

Parrying the right jab to the stomach with a simultaneous right jab

side view

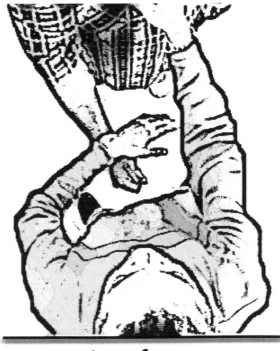

top view

Parrying the left jab to the stomach with a simultaneous left jab

side view

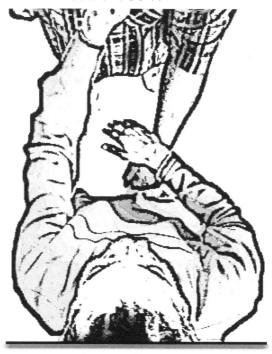

top view

189

Parrying the right hook to the obliques with a simultaneous right jab to the nose

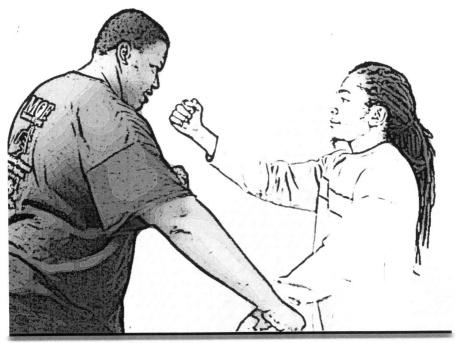

Parrying the right kick to the obliques with a simultaneous right jab to the nose

190

Parrying the left hook to the obliques with a simultaneous left jab to the nose

Parrying the left kick to the obliques with a simultaneous left jab to the nose

191

hands-together bow is a simple gesture that shows modesty and respect

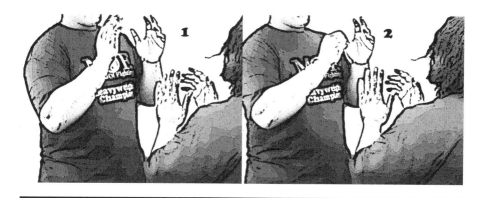

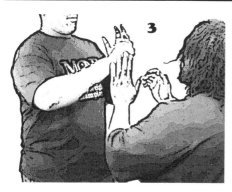

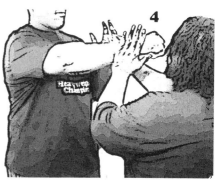

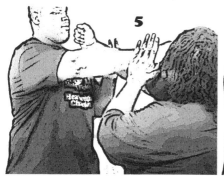

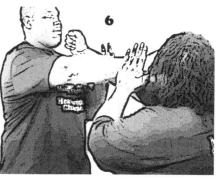

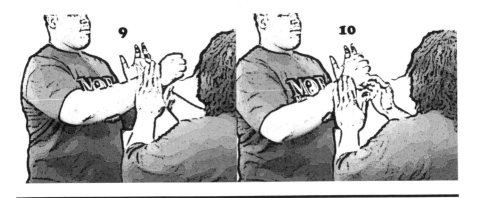

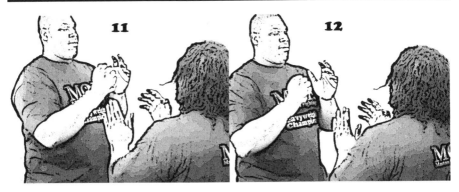

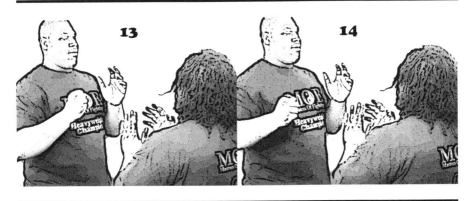

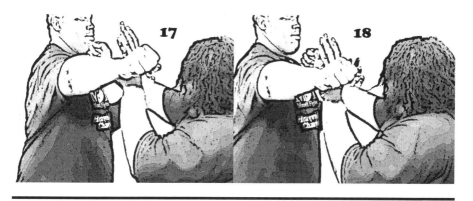

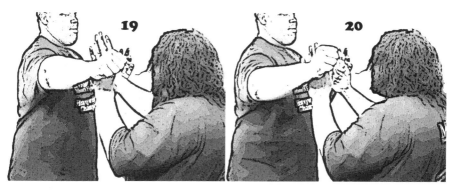

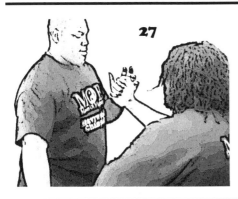

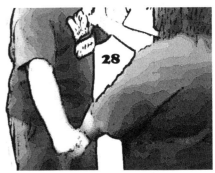

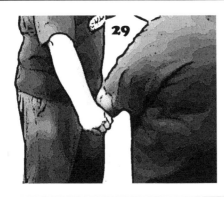

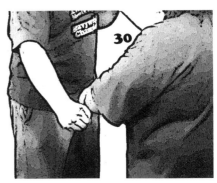

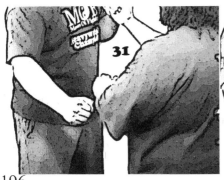

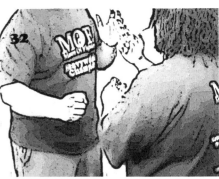

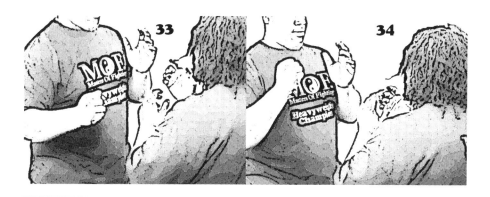

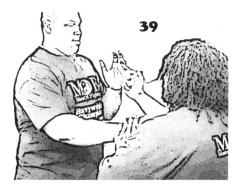
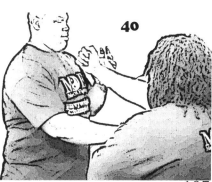

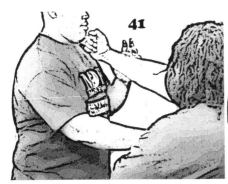

41

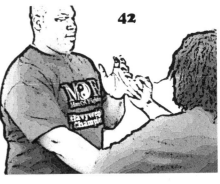

42

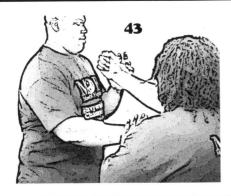

43

44

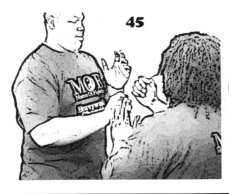

45

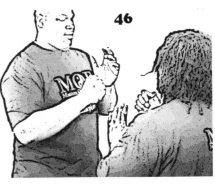

46

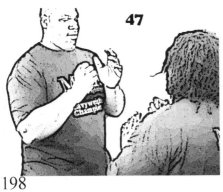

47

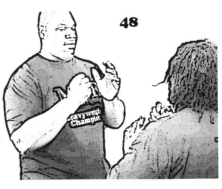

48

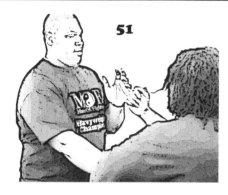

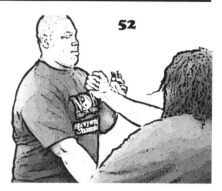

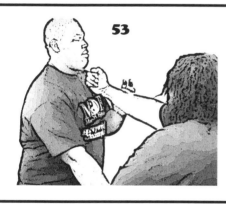

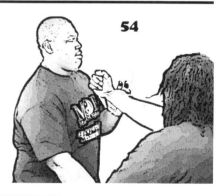

199

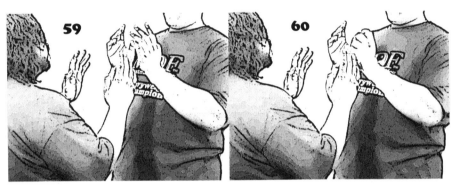

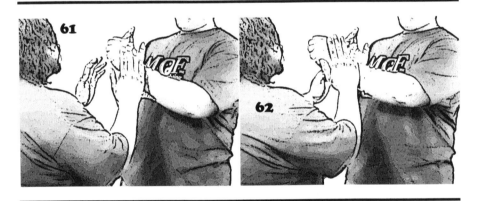

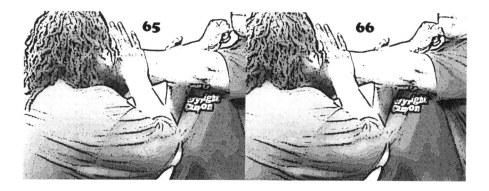

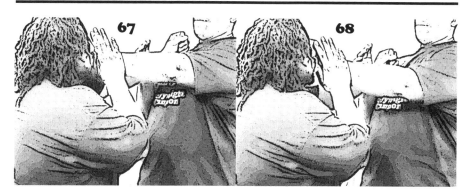

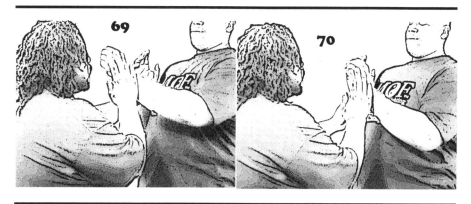

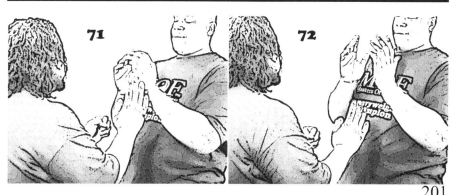

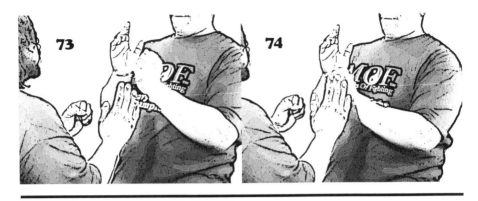

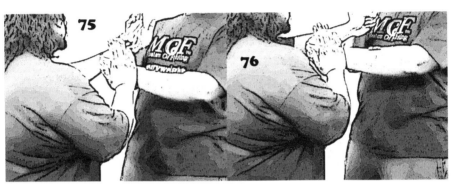

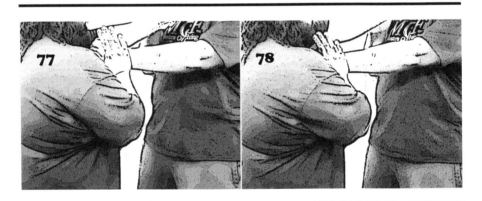

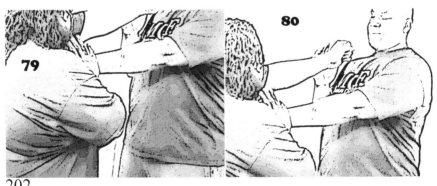

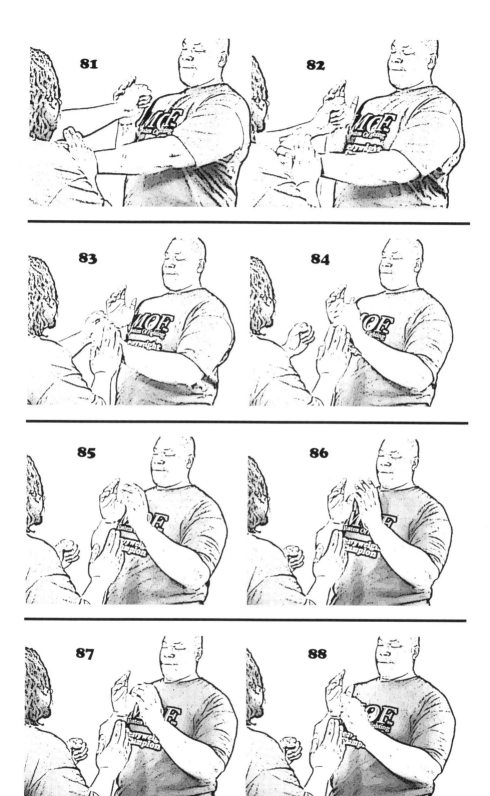

203

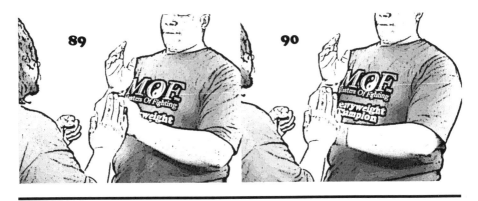

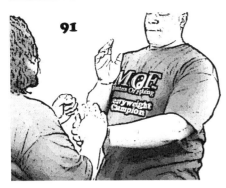

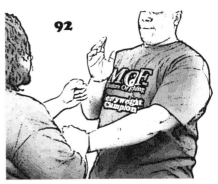

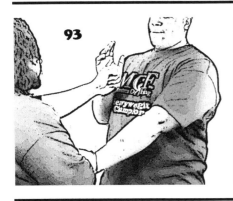

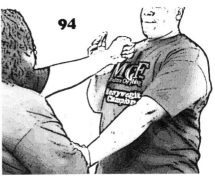

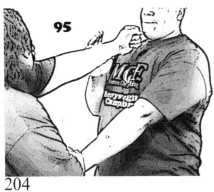

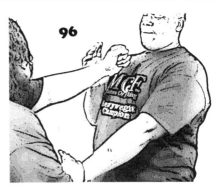

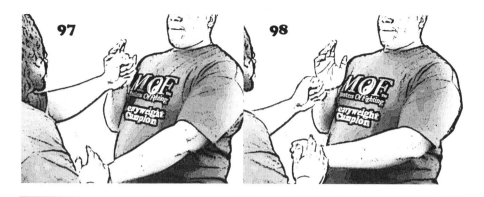

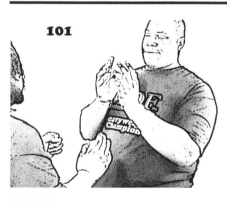

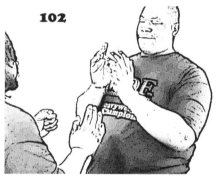

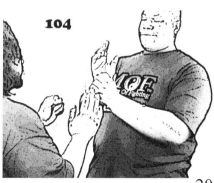

205

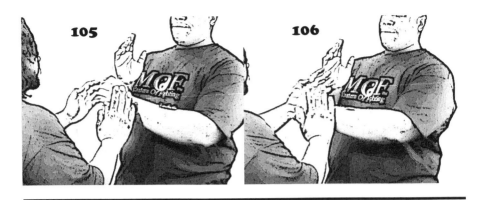

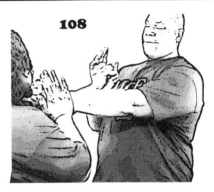

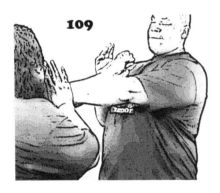

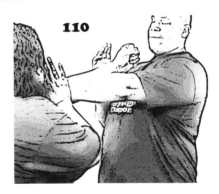

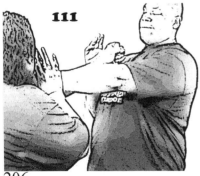

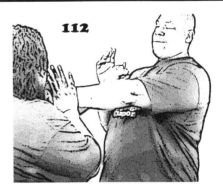

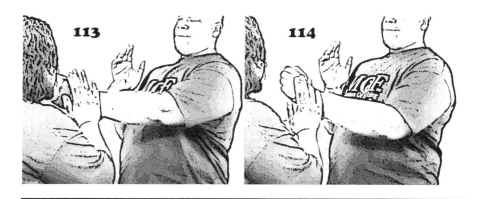

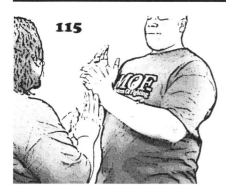

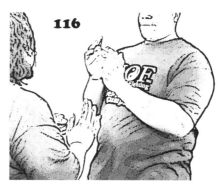

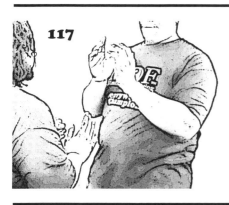

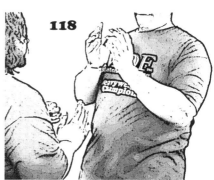

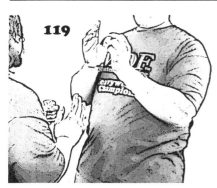

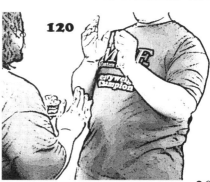

207

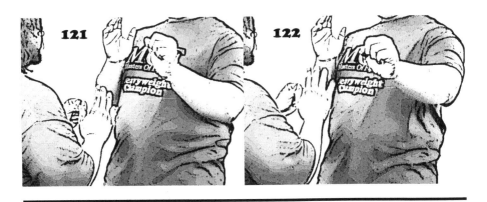

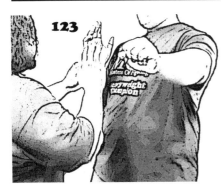

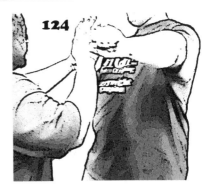

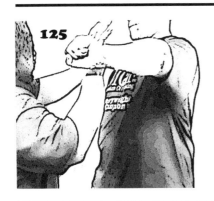

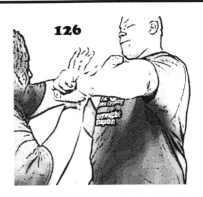

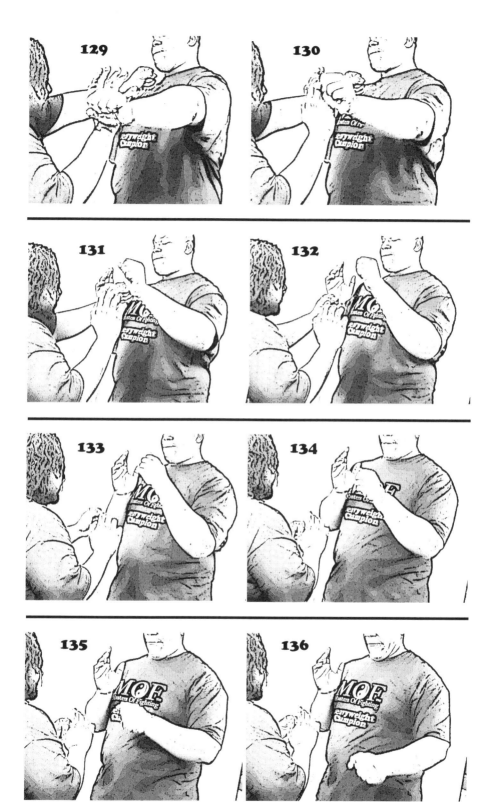

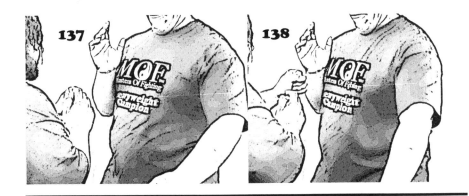

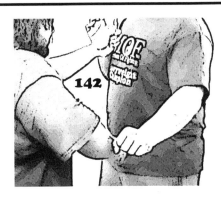

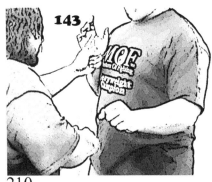

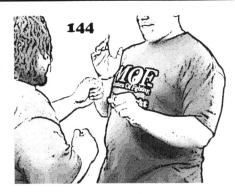

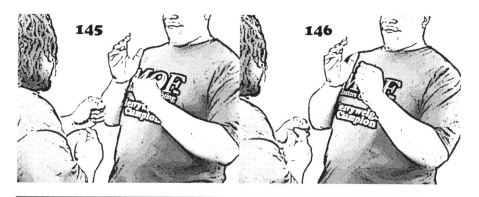

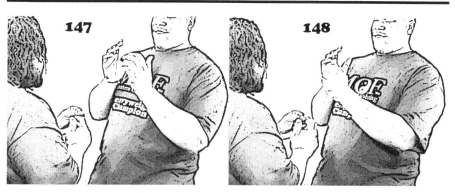

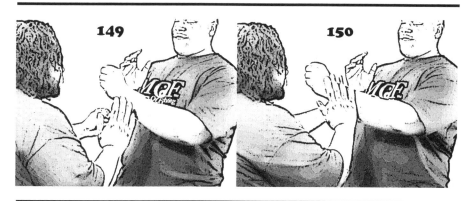

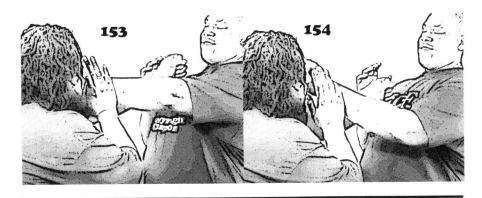

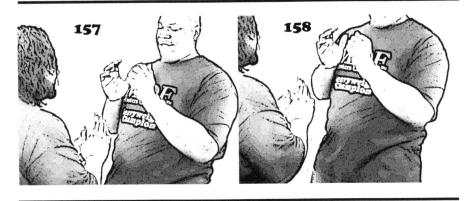

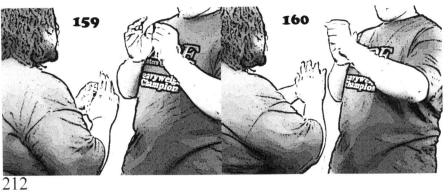

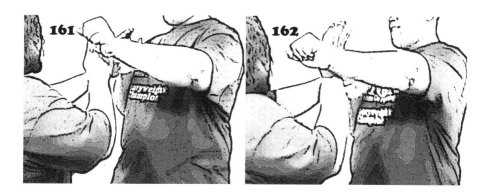

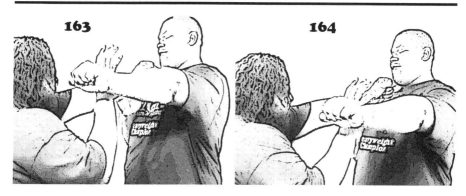

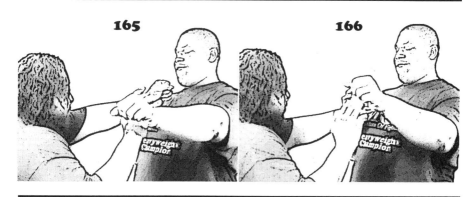

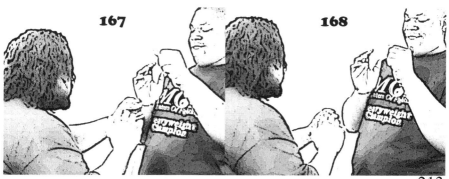

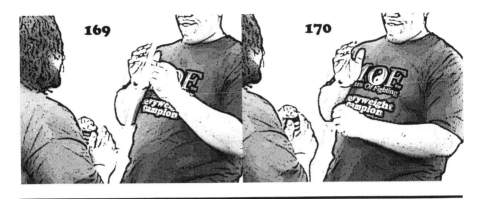

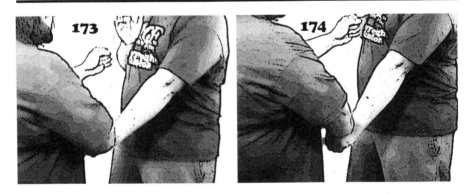

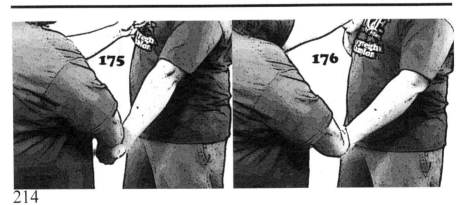

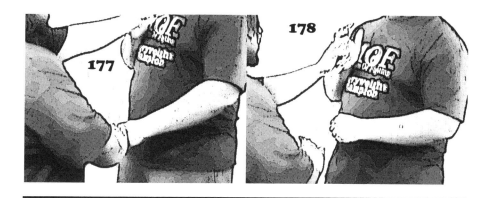

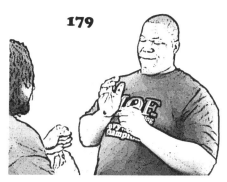

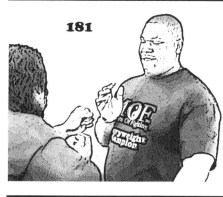

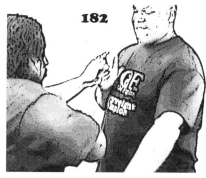

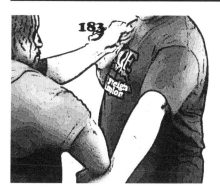

215

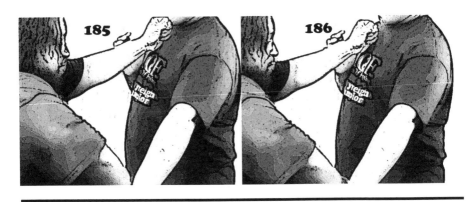

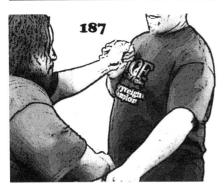

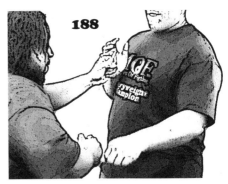

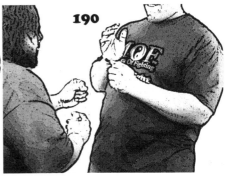

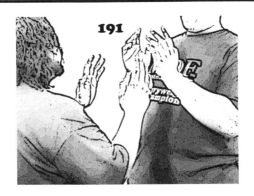

In the previous illustrations (1) to (58) show a part of the third drill looking over the left shoulder of the defender. The illustrations are showing only five attacks and parries each with a simultaneous jab. The punches thrown in order were a right jab to the nose, a right hook to the temple, a right hook to the obliques, a right jab to the chest, and a right jab to the abdomen. A hook to the ribs are not shown.

In the illustrations (59) to (191) the view is over the right shoulder of the master. These illustrations are just to give you an idea of what it should look like. The focus here is to build the ability to defend and attack simultaneously. In doing that, you need to learn the movements of the body before and during an attack. At the same time, get to know your reaction time. Pay close attention to the timing and distance of each attack. This practice with a real person will dramatically pay off in your ability to defend.

As the attacker in this drill, your focus should be on helping your partner get better at defense. Remember to always stay relaxed when throwing punches and stop three inches before you would make contact. You, also, should start off slow, and then gradually pick up speed as their defense gets better. You will, also, benefit from this drill because in every drill both percipients are building hand-and-eye coordination. Learning to better control their hands and fist from what they see and increasing the speed of doing so.

Getting The Most Benefit

It's time to get a few pointers to help you achieve the expected result which is mastering self-defense

Mastering Self-Defense

From The Drills
Mastering Self-Defense

Here are some things to remember while doing these drills. The first thing is to stay relaxed. Keep the use of energy to a minimum. Try not to ever stay tensed up because incorrect muscle usage will get you hit. Being tensed slows your hand-and-eye coordination. Also, remember to focus on your partner's whole body, from the top of the head to the tip of their feet. You must see everything that is going on. Training your eyes is part of building excellent hand-eye coordination. Remember to never waste movement by extending your parries past what is needed and never get upset with yourself for not reacting quickly enough, just relax and focus. It will get easier and it will start to feel natural. The goal is to do all that is necessary without having to think about anything. I call that programming the subconscious. Like I said before, you get good at something physical only by doing it. The more you do the better you get.

I found that having many partners of different heights and widths will increase your ability to defend an attack from anyone. A difference in height and width of your partner will affect the angles and the distance needed to strike and defend.

219

Teaching Your Partner

Now it's time to take your ability to another level and obtain a better understanding

Obtaining A Better Understanding

Teaching Your Partner

Taking You To Another Level

You must do these drills to achieve the goal of this book. After learning all this information and understanding how the drills work, you are ready to teach your partner. Your partner needs to learn how to stand, arm position, how to parry, and how to throw both types of punches.

Teach them about the use of energy and what distance to stop their punch. Show them and make sure they have a good understanding mentally and physically before starting any drill. Safety comes first! You or your partner should never get hurt or injured while doing any of these drills.

After teaching your partner and doing the drills in my process, look at your skill level and your new-found ability. I have seen the results many times and know how it changes the game.

The Conclusion

Your results from my process

The End Of The First Lesson

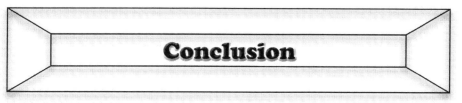

Conclusion

The End Of This Lesson

After completing my process and gaining the ability to go very fast doing all three the drills; you should come to a state of mind where you can consciously see everything your opponent is doing whether it's your training partner, for the sport or in the streets. You, also, should know how to parry and punch simultaneously, while reserving energy and increasing your speed, allowing you to strike your opponent whenever they try to attack. Due to your increased level of hand-and-eye coordination in fighting, this will be very easy. The truth of the matter is after completing the first lesson, these are the results of all my students and I sincerely want the same for you.

In my opinion, this is the first step to becoming a master of fighting and for many of you this lesson will be enough. This first lesson got you to your goals in fighting which is great! But for those of you who want to continue to master fighting and your skill level higher, look for my second lesson which is focused on learning to speed up your reaction time from what you feel. This is another level and a greater connection between mind and body. It's been a pleasure sharing this information with you and I hope that you get to where you want to be.

**Grandmaster Gary Howell, Jr. practicing on a
MOF Wing Chun training dummy**

About The Author

A Master Of Fighting

Gary Howell, Jr. has been the head instructor for Masters of Fighting Training Facility since 2014. His passion for helping people in all aspects of life flows through in the expert self-defense instruction he provides. In addition to teaching self-defense, Gary also provides higher levels of training for people in the sport of mixed martial arts and boxing, as well as specific types of training for law enforcement, security, body guards, and bouncers. For over thirty years he has been studying the philosophies and techniques used in fighting. The styles are too numerous to mention, but with one in particular, he has taught students how to strike an opponent thirty times in three seconds. He loves teaching martial arts as much as he loves practicing them.

71101092R00129

Made in the USA
Columbia, SC
20 May 2017